A Quick-Start Guide to

Building Assets in Your Prevention Program

by Deborah Fisher

Contents

2 Introduction: Building the Web of Support All Youth Need
   3 Building Assets Works
   4 40 Developmental Assets: Essentials for Helping Every Young Person Succeed
   6 The Power of Assets
   7 Using the Five Action Strategies to Transform Prevention Programs

8 Invigorate Programs
12 Engage Adults
16 Mobilize Young People
21 Activate Sectors
25 Influence Civic Decisions
27 Resources

INTRODUCTION:

Building the Web of Support All Youth Need

This book is for prevention-program leaders and staff in schools, youth and family-serving organizations, juvenile justice systems, and health-care settings who sometimes find themselves overwhelmed by programming demands, funding criteria, and statistics. Much of your work must focus, by necessity, on trying to prevent individual risk behaviors. We want to show you how Developmental Assets can be blended with prevention programs to build a broader, more effective core set of protective factors within young people.

What we're describing here is an approach, not a program in and of itself. Asset building is based on Search Institute's framework of 40 Developmental Assets—supportive conditions that help young people thrive. The framework (which you'll find on pages 4–5) describes a set of concrete, commonsense, positive experiences and qualities essential to raising successful young people. These assets, divided into eight categories for ease of understanding and use, have the power during critical adolescent years to influence choices young people make and help them become caring, responsible adults. **Research shows that young people who report having more Developmental Assets are less likely to abuse alcohol and other drugs or engage in violence and sexual activity.**

This book provides guidance on how to infuse assets into your prevention efforts. **We recommend integrating assets into existing programs rather than just adding them on.** Infusing assets into the work you're already doing can be a win-win situation all around: adults will be energized by a new, more optimistic outlook; youth will be empowered to make positive changes in their own lives.

Weaving assets into your program starts by refocusing the lens through which you view your work. Here's a table to help you think about what the shift from a deficit focus to an asset focus looks like:

Essential Shifts Needed to Build Assets for All Children and Young People	
From...	*To...*
Deficit language	Asset language
Focus only on youth identified as troubled	Focus on all children and young people
Focus on only one age group for intervention	Focus on all ages, from birth to 18
Age segregation	Intergenerational community
Self-interest	Shared responsibility
Buy and implement new programs	Infuse assets into existing programs
Fragmented agenda	Unifying vision around Developmental Assets
Youth as objects of programs	Working with and for youth in a change process
Constant switching of flavor-of-the-month priorities	Long-term commitment
Civic disengagement	Engaged public

Building Assets Works

Extensive research confirms the power of Developmental Assets in young people's lives. Search Institute has conducted more than 1,200 surveys of students in grades 6 through 12, and the results show that, regardless of gender, ethnic heritage, economic situation, or geographic location, the more assets young people have, the better they do in school and in many other areas, such as making healthy choices, exhibiting leadership, and valuing diversity.

Search Institute research also clearly demonstrates that the more assets young people have, the less likely they are to become involved in risky behaviors. **Increasing the number of Developmental Assets youth have is especially powerful in preventing or delaying the use of alcohol, tobacco, and other drugs (ATOD), and engagement in violence and sexual activity**.

It's important to encourage programs and communities to increase all of the categories of Developmental Assets for all youth, but we also know that certain categories of assets are more strongly related to lower levels of risk in certain key areas. For example, the Boundaries and Expectations asset category is most strongly related to lower levels of ATOD use while Constructive Use of Time and Commitment to Learning also seem to play a strong role in reducing high-risk behaviors.

We all want programs to be effective in achieving goals and outcomes, not just for the sake of science, but to know that we are truly making a difference in the lives of young people. New prevention research is documenting the evidence-base for proven programs, which means a program demonstrates consistently positive results through scientific study. **Power-packing proven programs with assets significantly increases your chances of success.**

What we're after here is something we call asset "pile-up." We want youth to experience lots of assets in lots of contexts throughout their lives. Consider research that shows the benefits of asset pile-up in these four critical ways:

- Youth who experience more assets in their families, schools, communities, and among peers do better than those who experience assets in fewer of these contexts *(horizontal accumulation)*.

- Youth who experience more assets throughout their lives are better equipped to navigate transitions *(vertical accumulation)*.

- Youth who repeatedly experience the same assets find that those assets renew and reinforce each other over time *(chronological accumulation)*.

- All children and youth benefit from the extended reach of intentional asset building, not just those judged to be "at risk" *(developmental breadth accumulation)*.

Clearly, prevention programs working alone, even those using assets and evidence-based strategies, cannot influence every area of young people's lives. We want to intentionally attempt to build the capacity of *all* communities, individuals, organizations, and networks to support young people's healthy development. This effort helps us address all the influences in young people's lives.

The tips, ideas, and strategies you'll find in this guide, when combined with your work and what we know about community building, can help you identify ways to connect with others and strengthen the impact of your programs.

40 Developmental Assets®
Essentials for Helping Every Young Person Succeed

Search Institute has identified the following building blocks of development
that help young people grow up healthy, caring, and responsible.

EXTERNAL ASSETS

SUPPORT
1. **Family Support**—Family life provides high levels of love and support.
2. **Positive Family Communication**—Young person and her or his parent(s) communicate positively, and young person is willing to seek advice and counsel from parent(s).
3. **Other Adult Relationships**—Young person receives support from three or more nonparent adults.
4. **Caring Neighborhood**—Young person experiences caring neighbors.
5. **Caring School Climate**—School provides a caring, encouraging environment.
6. **Parent Involvement in Schooling**—Parent(s) are actively involved in helping young person succeed in school.

EMPOWERMENT
7. **Community Values Youth**—Young person perceives that adults in the community value youth.
8. **Youth as Resources**—Young people are given useful roles in the community.
9. **Service to Others**—Young person serves in the community one hour or more per week.
10. **Safety**—Young person feels safe at home, at school, and in the neighborhood.

BOUNDARIES AND EXPECTATIONS
11. **Family Boundaries**—Family has clear rules and consequences and monitors the young person's whereabouts.
12. **School Boundaries**—School provides clear rules and consequences.
13. **Neighborhood Boundaries**—Neighbors take responsibility for monitoring young people's behavior.
14. **Adult Role Models**—Parent(s) and other adults model positive, responsible behavior.
15. **Positive Peer Influence**—Young person's best friends model responsible behavior.
16. **High Expectations**—Both parent(s) and teachers encourage the young person to do well.

CONSTRUCTIVE USE OF TIME
17. **Creative Activities**—Young person spends three or more hours per week in lessons or practice in music, theater, or other arts.
18. **Youth Programs**—Young person spends three or more hours per week in sports, clubs, or organizations at school and/or in the community.
19. **Religious Community**—Young person spends one or more hours per week in activities in a religious institution.
20. **Time at Home**—Young person is out with friends "with nothing special to do" two or fewer nights per week.

INTERNAL ASSETS

COMMITMENT TO LEARNING
21. **Achievement Motivation**—Young person is motivated to do well in school.
22. **School Engagement**—Young person is actively engaged in learning.
23. **Homework**—Young person reports doing at least one hour of homework every school day.
24. **Bonding to School**—Young person cares about her or his school.
25. **Reading for Pleasure**—Young person reads for pleasure three or more hours per week.

POSITIVE VALUES
26. **Caring**—Young person places high value on helping other people.
27. **Equality and Social Justice**—Young person places high value on promoting equality and reducing hunger and poverty.
28. **Integrity**—Young person acts on convictions and stands up for her or his beliefs.
29. **Honesty**—Young person "tells the truth even when it is not easy."
30. **Responsibility**—Young person accepts and takes personal responsibility.
31. **Restraint**—Young person believes it is important not to be sexually active or to use alcohol or other drugs.

SOCIAL COMPETENCIES
32. **Planning and Decision Making**—Young person knows how to plan ahead and make choices.
33. **Interpersonal Competence**—Young person has empathy, sensitivity, and friendship skills.
34. **Cultural Competence**—Young person has knowledge of and comfort with people of different cultural/racial/ethnic backgrounds.
35. **Resistance Skills**—Young person can resist negative peer pressure and dangerous situations.
36. **Peaceful Conflict Resolution**—Young person seeks to resolve conflict nonviolently.

POSITIVE IDENTITY
37. **Personal Power**—Young person feels he or she has control over "things that happen to me."
38. **Self-Esteem**—Young person reports having a high self-esteem.
39. **Sense of Purpose**—Young person reports that "my life has a purpose."
40. **Positive View of Personal Future**—Young person is optimistic about her or his personal future.

The 40 Developmental Assets® may be reproduced for educational, noncommercial uses only (with this copyright line). Copyright © 1997 by Search Institute®, Minneapolis, MN; 800-888-7828; www.search-institute.org.

The Power of Assets

On one level, the 40 Developmental Assets® represent common wisdom about the kinds of positive experiences and characteristics that young people need and deserve. But their value extends further. Surveys of more than 2 million young people in grades 6–12 have shown that assets are powerful influences on adolescent behavior. (The numbers below reflect 2003 data from 148,189 young people in 202 communities.) Regardless of gender, ethnic heritage, economic situation, or geographic location, these assets both promote positive behaviors and attitudes and help protect young people from many different problem behaviors.

0–10 ASSETS   11–20 ASSETS   21–30 ASSETS   31–40 ASSETS

Promoting Positive Behaviors and Attitudes

Search Institute research shows that the greater the number of assets students report having, the more likely they are to also report the following patterns of thriving behavior:

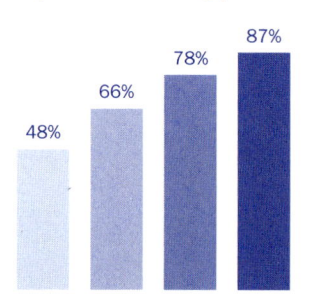

Exhibits Leadership — 48%, 66%, 78%, 87%
Has been a leader of an organization or group in the past 12 months.

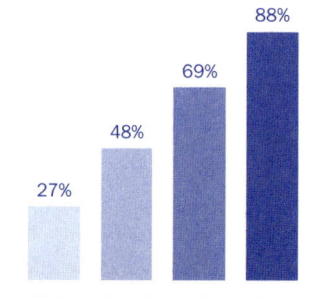

Maintains Good Health — 27%, 48%, 69%, 88%
Takes good care of body (such as eating foods that are healthy and exercising regularly).

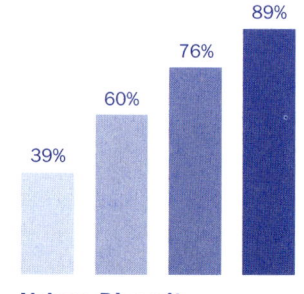

Values Diversity — 39%, 60%, 76%, 89%
Thinks it is important to get to know people of other racial/ethnic groups.

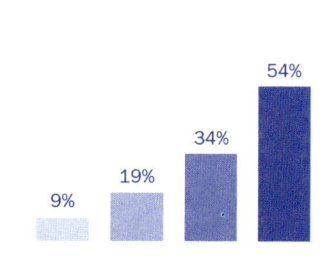

Succeeds in School — 9%, 19%, 34%, 54%
Gets mostly As on report card (an admittedly high standard).

Protecting Youth from High-Risk Behaviors

Assets not only promote positive behaviors, they also protect young people; the more assets a young person reports having, the less likely he or she is to make harmful or unhealthy choices. (Note that high-risk behaviors are defined in terms of multiple occurrences in order to distinguish between casual experimentation and more serious, ongoing problem behaviors.)

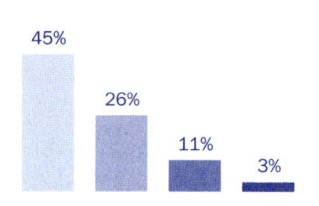

Problem Alcohol Use — 45%, 26%, 11%, 3%
Has used alcohol three or more times in the past 30 days or got drunk once or more in the past two weeks.

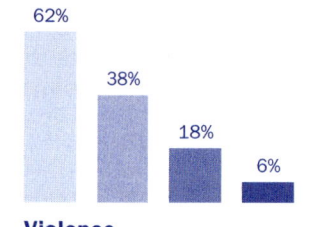

Violence — 62%, 38%, 18%, 6%
Has engaged in three or more acts of fighting, hitting, injuring a person, carrying a weapon, or threatening physical harm in the past 12 months.

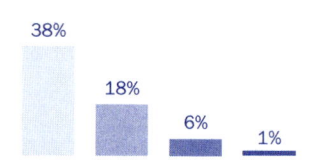

Illicit Drug Use — 38%, 18%, 6%, 1%
Used illicit drugs (marijuana, cocaine, LSD, PCP/angel dust, heroin, or amphetamines) three or more times in the past 12 months.

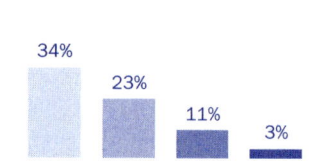

Sexual Activity — 34%, 23%, 11%, 3%
Has had sexual intercourse three or more times in lifetime.

Reprinted from *The Asset Approach: 40 Elements of Healthy Development*; copyright © 2006 by Search Institute®. This handout may be reproduced for educational, noncommercial uses only (with this copyright line). From *A Quick-Start Guide to Building Assets in Your Prevention Program*. Copyright © 2008 by Search Institute®, Minneapolis, MN; 800-888-7828, www.search-institute.org.

Using the Five Action Strategies to Transform Prevention Programs

Search Institute has identified **Five Action Strategies** (pictured below) for naming, encouraging, and linking all the important people, places, activities, and programs necessary to build a world where all young people are valued and thrive. The Five Action Strategies provide a practical framework to help you understand and describe how your work affects young people. As program leaders and community initiatives work to build assets and strengthen relationships within and among the spheres of influence shown in the Five Action Strategies graphic, they build a web of interconnected efforts. Merging the asset-building capacities of all community members increases our chances of success in making lasting, positive change.

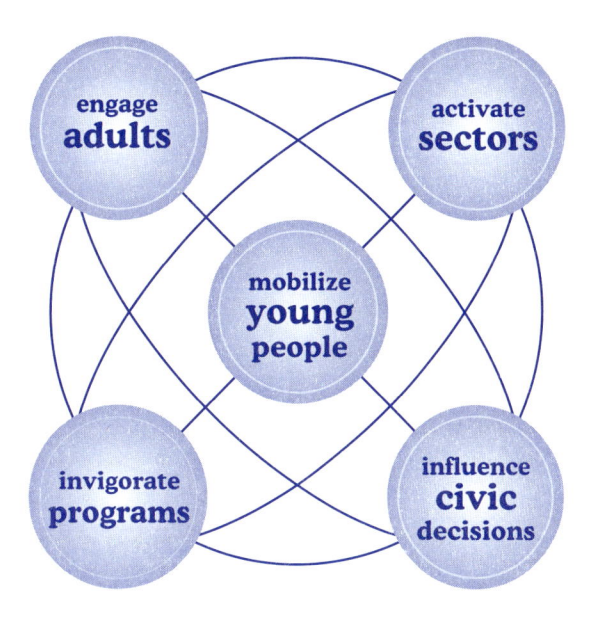

- engage **adults**
- activate **sectors**
- mobilize **young people**
- invigorate **programs**
- influence **civic decisions**

This guide uses the Five Action Strategies to illustrate ways you can incorporate the Developmental Assets into what you're already doing. In each section, you'll find:

- A brief summary of each Action Strategy
- Research, tips, and ideas for building assets in a variety of prevention programs
- Stories and practical examples illustrating how others are already using assets
- Where to find additional information or other useful resources

The overarching strategies we've embedded in this book emphasize the importance of:

- Building strong relationships *with* and *for* young people
- Creating multiple, positive environments to surround youth
- Enhancing programs and practices using proven, concrete methods

Unless otherwise noted, the research cited in this book comes from Search Institute studies.

Invigorate Programs

What This Means
Invigorate, expand, and enhance programs to become more asset rich and to be available to and accessed by all children and youth.

The Goal
Inspire your own organizations and assist others to infuse asset building into cultures, programs, and practices.

Programs that share a common, asset-enhanced vision and that send strong messages about expectations and values to youth provide a powerful web of support for young people. You can find ways within your programs and organizations to power-pack your work with assets. You can also find new, creative ways to join forces with others in the community to deliver your work in complementary, resource-efficient ways. Consider these strategies:

IDENTIFY WHAT YOU'RE ALREADY DOING—Sit down with the asset framework and create a list of the ones you're already building. Share this list! Ask others to add their insights.

IDENTIFY WHICH ASSETS YOU "OWN"—Be clear about which assets your program can actually build. Schools or alcohol or other drug prevention programs may each "own" some assets more than others.

IDENTIFY WHERE TO STACK UP ASSETS—Infuse assets in creative and inexpensive ways. Some examples include making asset building part of job descriptions or infusing asset language into existing curricula.

Combining assets with proven prevention programs can make a meaningful difference in the lives of young people, but sometimes, evidence-based programs cost a lot of money, or they don't fit for youth in your community. How should you proceed?

USE AN EXISTING PROGRAM—Try to find a program already developed in your topic area that's been evaluated and shown to be successful with youth similar to yours.

ADAPT AN EXISTING PROGRAM—If a program doesn't exist or the costs are too high, you might be able to carefully borrow, model, or replicate successful programs using best practices.

DESIGN YOUR OWN INNOVATION—Practitioners can and do develop new programs and strategies using best practices. Local innovations should meet generally accepted criteria for effective programs before being implemented or disseminated.

Here are ideas and activities you can use to invigorate your prevention programs and strategies.

SCHOOLS

A study of 104 schools in 12 states found that many are adopting research-based curricula according to the U.S. Department of Education's Principles of Effectiveness, but only 19 percent were implementing the curricula with fidelity. To improve the quality and performance of your programs:

- Make sure teachers are adequately trained in the curriculum (or retrained if necessary)
- Make sure all classes using a curriculum have access to it
- Make sure that a complete set of curriculum materials is used when classes are taught

Researchers looking at a diverse sampling of adolescents in nine California and Wisconsin high schools found higher levels of protection against delinquency and substance use among youth who experienced a group or "cluster" of assets. The students:

- Experienced warm relations with parents
- Came from relatively well-organized households
- Valued academic achievements
- Engaged in school, felt close to teachers, and performed well in school

YOUTH-SERVING ORGANIZATIONS

Many youth-serving organizations are infusing assets into their work and monitoring their results, including 4-H, Boys and Girls Clubs, Girl Scouts, and Big Brothers Big Sisters. The YMCA conducted its own study, asking the question, "How does the *Abundant Assets Initiative* affect the institutional culture of the YMCA?" Some of the answers included:

NAMING AND TELLING—The initiative's use of asset language gives the Y more concrete ways of describing its impact.

VERIFYING AND PRIORITIZING—Asset research helps staff focus and demonstrates to staff, funders, and community stakeholders that programs make a difference.

MEASURING AND REINFORCING—The Y and its partners can better see the impact of its investment.

Here's an example of how one YMCA boosted its asset impact in an urban community:

Find Out More

To learn more about evidence-based programs and best practices to help you adapt or design your own work:

National Registry of Evidence-based Programs and Practices
nrepp.samhsa.gov

Blueprints for Violence Prevention
colorado.edu/cspv/blueprints

Centers for Disease Control
Best Practices of Youth Violence Prevention: A Sourcebook for Community Action
cdc.gov

Family Dinners Have Power

Parade magazine reported these startling results of several studies:

- Teens who eat regular meals with their family earn better grades and are less depressed (University of Minnesota).

- Children are 15 percent less likely to be overweight if they eat meals with their families (Harvard University).

- Preteens whose parents tell family stories at dinner report higher self-esteem and better peer relations through adolescence (Emory University).

- Teens who eat five or more family dinners a week are less likely to smoke, drink, and hang out with sexually active friends (National Center on Addiction and Substance Abuse, Columbia University).

Chairman and president of the National Center on Addiction and Substance Abuse, Joseph A. Califano Jr., cited family dinners as better than any law or punishments, saying, "Parental engagement is a critical weapon in the fight against substance abuse."

....

The YMCA in Bellevue, Washington, had been regularly opening its facilities for free one Friday night a month to low-income or new-to-the-community families. A small local grant allowed them to also provide free meals for about 25 people. The Bellevue Parks and Recreation Department was looking for a way to support more asset building in the community without starting new projects. A brainstorming session of local asset builders came up with Family Friendly Fridays. The city kicked in additional money to the Y to feed up to 100 people, and volunteers gave short talks at each of the Friday dinners on asset-oriented topics such as how to involve children in planning and eating nutritious meals together and different ways to celebrate holidays. Young people also helped present some of the programs. Attendance was packed for each event.

FAMILY-SERVING ORGANIZATIONS

Pioneer Camp is a Lutheran retreat center in Angola, New York. Among the many activities it offers is the Papyrus Program for children in foster care, who sometimes have only five days at camp as a transition between foster homes. The challenge of infusing assets into a short-term program was met by using some of these strategies:

FOCUS—Clear, obtainable objectives with simple outcomes were written for each of the eight asset categories, such as making sure that all staff say hello to each child so that campers come away from their experience with a greater sense of personal identity.

TRAINING—*All* staff connected to the camp learned about asset building, from the 16-year-old lifeguards to the board members.

ACCOUNTABILITY—Staff checked in at every meeting to report the number of children they had greeted that day and the quality of the responses they got.

CURRICULUM—New asset-infused games were developed and assets were inserted into existing activities, such as daily "Cabin Time."

EVALUATION—Camp staff worked with Search Institute to develop simple evaluation forms such as a short survey, counselor response forms, observation and daily logs, and a follow-up phone survey.

JUVENILE JUSTICE

It might seem more difficult to build assets in programs and settings when youth appear to be unreachable or are in crisis. But who needs asset building more than young people in crisis? "They probably don't have control over their lives," says writer and curriculum developer Neal Starkman. "Identifying what they *can* do as opposed to what they can't is an important step on the road to building those assets. What better haven in a crisis than the ability and confidence to rely on your own strengths?"

Michael Clark agrees. A former juvenile probation officer, Clark now runs the Center for Strength-Based Strategies, which promotes strength-based practices across all helping professions through training and technical assistance. "When we use asset-building approaches in child welfare, juvenile delinquency, or adolescent substance abuse work, we still try to resolve problems just like any other approach, but instead of fixating on problems and failure, we focus on the hopes, dreams, proclivities, wants, desires, and talents of those who are troubled," says Clark. Some of Clark's suggestions:

CHANGE FOCUS—Incorporate asset assessment in intakes and interviews to help map out a path for change; ask young people to identify their strengths as well as their dreams, then help them achieve them.

INCLUDE FAMILY—Staff should share the "expert" role with youth and family.

FIND OUT WHAT'S WORKED—Asking youth about what has helped and not helped will give you lots of useful information.

Clark also advocates quickly checking in with youth after every conversation to see if they feel they're being listened to, that issues discussed were important to them, and if they liked what they did that day. The advantage: staff can quickly assess if there's a relationship problem and fix it.

HEALTH

Several programs are getting good results in promoting healthy teen relationships using Developmental Assets in their curricula as well as in how they deliver their programs.

The Arizona-based nonprofit Peer Solutions concentrates on uniting schools, families, and communities to reduce harmful behaviors. One of the chief aims of its Stand & Serve program is reducing sexual, dating, family, and gang violence. The program concentrates on building several asset areas—respect, communication, responsibility, social competencies—to achieve its goals.

A key to the program's success so far is the leadership roles played by youth who deliver the program to their peers through:

- Weekly meetings with discussions and projects at high schools before school, during lunch, and after school
- Weekly peer education workshops at middle schools after school
- Monthly training; peer mentor projects with elementary students; and school, family, and community awareness and resource referral campaigns

A sample of evaluation results from participants showed that the program improves youths' understanding of violence, their respect for others, and their ability to resolve conflict and help others.

The Virginia-based Teens Against Sexual Assault (TASA) program is a volunteer group that educates communities about healthy relationships and works to stop dating violence and sexual assault. Teens designed their own peer education manual and brochures, including quizzes for males and females called "How healthy is your relationship?" Teachers support the program by letting teens have time away from school to give presentations, and adults involved in supporting the teen educators say evaluations are better and volunteer recruitment is higher when teens are running the show. Why? Students who can answer questions more candidly from their own experiences with the issues are seen as live resources in their schools. Said one teen about what she learned from her peers, "It makes the information seem more real."

Find Out More

Pioneer Camp
pioneercamp.org

Find Out More

Center for Strength-Based Strategies
buildmotivation.com

Find Out More

Both of these programs are described in *Moving Upstream,* Virginia's Newsletter for the Primary Prevention of Sexual & Intimate Partner Violence.
vsdvalliance.org

Engage Adults

What This Means
Engage adults from all walks of life to develop sustained, strength-building relationships with children and adolescents, both within families and in neighborhoods.

The Goal
Build as many relationships between youth and positive adults as possible.

Relationships of all kinds provide the energy that animates the Developmental Assets framework. The power of every single one of the 40 assets is enhanced when you make building relationships an essential ingredient of your work. Search Institute president Peter Benson writes in *All Kids Are Our Kids,* "Of all the assets, it may well be that adult relationships—particularly for teenagers—generate more asset-building energy than any other developmental resource." Here's what research tells us are the benefits:

- Supportive relationships with adults erect a protective buffer against risk behaviors.
- Relationships become more powerful the longer they're sustained.
- The more relationships youth have with positive adults, the better.

Let's look at some activities you can use to engage more adults in asset building and strengthen your prevention strategies.

SCHOOLS

When St. Louis Park High School in Minnesota decided to tackle alarming increases in 9th-grade truancy, academic failure, and alcohol and other drug use, staff concentrated on integrating the asset categories proven to help reduce risky behaviors as well as promote thriving interactions. The 9th-grade program that emerged focused on bolstering Support, Boundaries and Expectations, Social Competencies, and Positive Identity asset categories.

The main vehicle for delivering the risk prevention program was an emphasis on relationship building between all incoming 9th graders and positive adult role models. To do this, a federal three-year State Incentive Grant (SIG) was used to:

INCREASE TIME—Class sizes were reduced and core subjects reorganized into longer blocks so teachers could have more sustained time with students.

INCREASE CONNECTIONS—Staff met with every incoming 9th grader to get acquainted. A simple "strengths and needs" assessment was done with each student, focusing on activities they were interested in doing while in high school. Staff made sure every student got connected to his or her desired activities.

INCREASE SKILLS—A new curriculum called "I Time" was developed to help build communication skills and social competencies. For 30 minutes every week, teachers and students participated in team-building activities. Teachers received training in the new curriculum.

INCREASE SUPPORT—Staff teams consisting of administrators, counselors, and teachers met weekly to discuss each 9th-grade student and focus on those needing additional support. Parents were also encouraged to become more positively involved with the school.

The program documented gains by the end of its first year, including upticks in areas of academic and social competence due, in part, to additional resources that allowed support staff to work with students of greatest need while freeing teachers to focus on the remaining majority of students. The project's regular meetings gave school staff, administrators, the student assistance team, project coordinator, and teachers a way to deal with crises and challenges for students as they occurred. Because of the positive trend in results the first year—and because teachers viewed the project as responsive to their concerns about 9th graders—teachers started lobbying the school board right away (successfully) for funding to keep the program going when the federal grant ran out.

Find Out More

For a complete set of logic models, process, and summative evaluation reports on the St. Louis Park 9th-grade program, go to cehd.umn.edu/CAREI/reports/sig, click on Evaluation Plans and Grantee Reports on the left side of the page, then scroll down to St. Louis Park.

YOUTH-SERVING ORGANIZATIONS

Youth-serving organizations have a unique opportunity to "up the asset ante." First, there's ample evidence to back up the claim that youth involvement in programs reduces the chances they'll engage in risky behaviors. Second, program staff have a number of opportunities to develop positive relationships with all kinds of young people of different ages and backgrounds. Third, youth-serving programs can also recruit other adults to participate as volunteers, creating the potential for young people to develop still more much-needed relationships.

Here are some ideas to help you multiply the benefits of adult-youth relationships in your organizations:

PROVIDE LEADERSHIP IN SMALL AND BIG WAYS—Search Institute findings reported in "Sorting Out What Makes a Difference" identify the importance of working with staff to ensure that youth get a variety of opportunities to make decisions within youth programs. Helping youth feel more comfortable accomplishing small tasks increases a sense of connection to the organization as they grow up and develop more leadership skills.

MAKE IT EASY FOR OTHER ADULTS TO GET INVOLVED—In a U.S. study called *Grading Grownups,* adults identified actions they believed were important to take with youth, such as having meaningful conversations or teaching respect for cultural differences. However, many also reported their reluctance to do these things, leaving a big gap between what adults said and what they actually did. You can offer adult volunteers the chance to act on their beliefs by inviting them to engage with youth in your programs, and ease the process by assigning specific tasks with clear expectations.

FAMILY-SERVING ORGANIZATIONS

Many family-serving organizations have successfully engaged parents and other adults by showing the natural connections between assets and different cultures. For example, native communities throughout Alaska contributed hundreds of village-specific ideas to the book *Helping Kids Succeed: Alaskan Style.*

Volunteers in Colorado work with Spanish-speaking parents, using the proverbs they grew up with, known as *dichos,* to help them make the cultural connection to the asset framework. "Once parents begin to see that their own parents and grandparents transmitted similar asset messages from one generation to another through *dichos,* they begin to understand the process and importance of intentionally building assets in their families, schools, and communities," says Patsy Roybal of the Colorado Statewide Parent Coalition.

Roybal and others use *dichos* as the basis for:

BUILDING A WEB OF SUPPORT—Parents are led through an exercise to identify not only what they will do to help ensure that *every* student in their school will experience success, but what other parents, staff, and community members can do, too.

CREATIVELY SHARING THE ASSET MESSAGE—A group of Spanish-speaking moms called *Flores Índigenas* formed around the idea of sharing *dichos* in a bilingual presentation that incorporates song, dance, stories, and narration. Children dance with their parents during the presentation, which features authentic Mexican dresses on which the eight asset categories are artistically portrayed and linked to *dichos* to help participants make the cultural connection. For example, the Positive Values category is promoted through the *dicho* "Live in such a way that when your children think of justice, love, and integrity, they will think of you."

JUVENILE JUSTICE

The YMCA in Victoria, Australia, runs several Y programs seven days a week inside juvenile justice centers. The Visiting Community Group program helps young people in custody prepare gradually for a return to community life through regular contact with positive adult role models. Community volunteers are invited to play team games with youth.

The program as originally conceived had been viewed as a success, but staff thought applying assets more intentionally would improve its outcomes. In particular, they realized that there wasn't much interaction going on between visitors and youth once games were done. Here's how they tweaked the program:

- A young person was selected to be a team representative to welcome visitors.
- The sports teams were mixed up so youth and adults were playing together.
- A social element with drinks and snacks was added at the end of the game.

Find Out More

Colorado Statewide Parent Coalition
coparentcoalition.org

- After each visit, different young people got the chance to thank visitors.
- Community teams were invited to visit several times in succession.

Says Sherilyn Hanson, the Y's Youth Justice and Forensics director, "To see a young person with not much confidence thank a team of volunteers for making the effort to come and visit them—and invite them back again—was really a joyful experience." Hanson reports that intentionally adding assets has not only benefited youth but also given the program more asset-rich material to use in reports and grant applications.

HEALTH

One prevention program has found great success combating childhood obesity by making participation as easy as possible for adults and children. The Tennessee Governor's Council on Physical Fitness and Health, the Tennessee Department of Health, and BlueCross BlueShield of Tennessee have teamed up to create BlueCross Walking Works for Schools, a program to encourage physical activity in elementary schools.

The program requires teachers to incorporate a minimum of five minutes of walking into each school day for a period of 12 weeks each semester. The teachers get basic materials to make it easier for them to participate such as pedometers to record the number of steps taken, tracking posters that chart class progress, information packets, and wristbands and achievement certificates to increase excitement and participation. Schools that reach a certain level of involvement receive recognition and big banners to display. Here are some of the key findings from evaluation of the program's first two years:

SIMPLICITY AS THE CORE APPEAL—The program set realistic goals for teachers and students of just five minutes of walking every day. Teachers were only asked to complete a 10-question survey every 12 weeks and materials they needed to promote the program were easily accessible on a Web site (walkingworksforschoolstn.com). Simplicity has also made replication and sustainability easier.

COLLABORATION CREATED A BETTER PROGRAM—The initial partnership between the state, schools, and BlueCross BlueShield attracted other partners such as the state's Department of Education as well as university and corporate interests that all added elements to the program's success. The Department of Education's contacts and credibility, for example, helped gain wider access to more schools for better implementation.

Evaluations gathered from participating teachers in the first year showed improved classroom behavior, improved attention span, increased energy levels, improved learning readiness, increased physical endurance, and some weight loss.

Find Out More

This and other programs are described in the online report *Childhood Obesity: Harnessing the Power of Public and Private Partnerships,* available at nihcm.org/pdf/FINAL_report_CDC_CO.pdf.

Mobilize Young People

What This Means
Mobilize young people to use their power as asset builders and change agents.

The Goal
Increase youth voice and engagement in every aspect of your work.

Everyone wants to feel valued and valuable. Too often, however, young people are identified as problems. Program funders or other stakeholders frequently require program designs and reports to have a deficit focus, forcing even well-intentioned programs to concentrate primarily on risk behaviors or "fixing" youth. But many deficit-focused prevention programs have designed ways to use asset building to reduce risk while also increasing protective factors. **One powerful strategy for accomplishing this task is to find as many ways as possible to increase youth voice and involvement in every aspect of your work.**

Developmental psychologist Peter Scales, Ph.D., has examined youth engagement issues in numerous studies for Search Institute, concluding that Empowerment and Social Competencies categories are optimal targets for increasing assets in young adolescents. "Many young adolescents want, and are ready for, more responsibility and chances to play meaningful roles but don't get enough opportunities," writes Scales. Show young people their value by providing them opportunities to:

- Make decisions and help set rules
- Govern themselves
- Resolve conflicts through peer mediation
- Develop their own initiatives with peers and other adults for solving school or community problems
- Ensure they have opportunities to serve others

Here are some strategies for mobilizing and engaging young people in your prevention efforts.

SCHOOLS

In a study done by the U.S. government's Substance Abuse and Mental Health Services Administration (SAMHSA) that examined the connection between youth activities, substance use, and family income, some interesting findings emerged:

- More than 92 percent of surveyed youth ages 12 to 17 reported participation in one or more activities through their school, community, or faith-based organization.

- Regardless of family income, the greater the number of activities in which youth were involved, the lower the rate of reported cigarette, alcohol, or other drug use.

It's clear that involvement in lots of different activities has a positive effect on youth. Schools can power-pack their activities with some of these asset-building extras:

INCLUDE CHILDREN IN PARENT-TEACHER CONFERENCES—Elementary school teachers using this strategy in Malverne, New York, and Chula Vista, California, report that children are more accountable for their behavior, and parents are more connected to their child's school. The Center on School, Family, and Community Partnerships found that parents are more likely to attend school conferences if their children have to come, and young people also benefit from the goal-setting that takes place.

PUT THEM IN CHARGE—The Teen Center in Essex, Vermont, is run by teens who develop the programs, oversee the budget, and hire (and fire) staff. Two school-centered youth governing boards are in charge of the center—one at the high school level and a second one at the middle school level, which also acts as a training ground. Adults are involved as trusted advisors. Young people gain confidence and learn to lead on the job, as well as discover new talents in themselves that influence positive life choices.

CHANGE PERSPECTIVE ON MENTORING—Many successful programs connect youth with adult mentors, but young people themselves are an untapped resource when it comes to mentoring. Schools have experienced success when youth run homework clubs for elementary-age children and help senior citizens learn how to use e-mail and the Internet. These activities have changed adult *and* youth perceptions of youth.

GO OUT AND TALK TO YOUTH—One high school principal invited a group of youth out for coffee and asked what it would take to get them involved in an activity. Reluctant at first, the teens eventually entered the conversation and defined their own mentoring program, backed by the school, that involved ski trips and learning how to install car stereos from local adults. The program increased connections with previously unconnected youth, leading to new opportunities for their growth.

YOUTH-SERVING ORGANIZATIONS

Sometimes there are barriers to developing meaningful youth-adult relationships. Both youth and adults can have preconceived notions about each other or have difficulty understanding each other's language or views. Often, youth and adults share the same concerns, but those concerns might be defined a bit differently. Here are some ideas to help you better engage youth:

Involving Ethnically Diverse Youth

Consider these principles from Assets for Colorado Youth (ACY) when engaging ethnically diverse youth:

1. *Culture influences behavior, but it doesn't determine behavior.* While there are shared qualities and experiences within ethnic groups, it's important to remember there is also diversity within ethnic groups.

2. *Relationships are key.* People change people. Strength-based relationships provide a platform for skill development, behavioral change, and informed decision making.

3. *Culture influences worldview.* This is true for providers as well as participants. Youth (and adults) may not be able to articulate the influences of culture, but that doesn't mean it should be ignored. **Naming and sharing cultural experiences allows for worldviews to be more meaningfully understood.**

Find Out More

Assets for Colorado Youth
buildassets.org

....

Find Out More

Leader to Leader Institute has resources for strengthening social leadership, including an *Innovation of the Week* e-newsletter.
leadertoleader.org

....

REACH THEM WHERE THEY LIVE—Caring adults in one rural community wanted to provide homework help to teens, and assumed that the best time and place would be after-hours at local schools. But a quick survey of youth revealed they were spending more of their free time at the local truck stop, so adult volunteers set up a tutoring station there instead.

KEEP AN OPEN MIND ABOUT WHAT *COMMUNITY* MEANS—Adults have good reason to be concerned about the increasing youth involvement in virtual communities and online social networks like Second Life® and Facebook, but their importance to many young people shouldn't be dismissed. "For many teenagers, virtual and social networks are more often tied to the intentional creation of their own personal community in their daily lives," says Lee Rush, executive director of *just*Community, Inc.

DIVERSITY IS A BIG ISSUE—But it doesn't quite mean the same thing to adults as it does to youth. When adults think of diversity, they think more of racial and ethnic issues. Youth tend to think more in terms of economics, sexual orientation, and social diversity. Providing opportunities for adults and youth to have meaningful conversations about these issues and differences in perception builds all sorts of important assets including Positive Family Communication, Community Values Youth, and Cultural Competence.

One organization's approach to helping youth express their ideas about diversity involves bringing the arts to rural communities. In a partnership between the Maine Alliance for Arts Education (MAAE) and 16 underserved high schools, Building Community Through the Arts (BCTA) sends outstanding professional Maine playwrights and choreographers experienced in working with teens into high school classrooms for two weeks. With teacher support, the visiting artists help all the students in the class create a short work of drama or dance based on their own self-identified issues. They don't use any pre-established materials; all the work is created collaboratively. Participating classes gather at a regional conference to share their work, reflect, and talk. Classes explore issues such as peer pressure, social harassment, homophobia, and frustration with life in rural towns. Some of the results:

- Students report a greater sense of community and higher levels of comfort with others.

- Measurable increases are evident in the percentage of students getting along better and feeling more respect for each other.

FAMILY-SERVING ORGANIZATIONS

A study done by the Pew Internet and American Life Project and the University of Illinois at Urbana-Champaign surprised researchers when it revealed that young adults are the heaviest users of public libraries. Despite how "wired" we think young people are, they still turn to libraries in larger numbers than older adults for additional help in finding information on health conditions, job training, government benefits, and other topics.

Besides boosting the Reading for Pleasure asset, many libraries actively engage young people in various asset-rich ways. The Fort Vancouver Regional Library District in Washington state has been intentional in regularly asking staff at trainings to brainstorm program ideas for building assets in young library patrons. Some activities include:

YOUNG ADULT ADVISORY BOARDS—Teens provide their input on library services, help plan programs, and do volunteer projects to support the library. Crucial to the library districts' credibility with teens is that no action is taken without a youth vote first.

JOINT PROJECTS WITH OTHER YOUTH-SERVING ORGANIZATIONS—Libraries work with parks and recreation departments, youth suicide prevention programs, schools, the YMCA, and local businesses. One especially important connection is outreach to the juvenile detention center, which includes book discussion groups on site as well as opportunities for teens to perform court-ordered community service at the library.

YOUTH-FRIENDLY, NONTRADITIONAL PROGRAMS—Libraries take an active role in hosting and organizing poetry slams, bowling nights, writing contests, and a battle of the bands. Especially popular is the Backlight Film Festival featuring student-produced films shown at a local theater.

JUVENILE JUSTICE

There are many ways juvenile justice programs are actively engaging youth—particularly through the use of youth courts. Youth courts are programs in which youth ages 11 to 18 are sentenced by their peers for a variety of offenses, including theft, alcohol and other drug use, assault, and truancy. Since the U.S. Department of Justice initiated the Federal Youth Court Program in 1997, the number of youth courts has grown to 1,255 in 49 states and the District of Columbia. Youth courts benefit both the young people being sentenced as well as those volunteering as peer attorneys and judges. The impact also extends deep into the community. For example:

- Wrangell, Alaska, reported that the community's juvenile delinquency rate dropped 30 percent in a four-year period. Also documented: measurable decreases in youth using alcohol and other drugs, attending drinking parties, and engaging in sexual activity.

- Youth-court adjudicated young people do better in school and many continue their education.

- Community service hours—for both court-involved youth and volunteers—go up significantly. Research shows that young people who volunteer are more likely to continue doing so into adulthood.

- Youth courts offer communities a swifter response to delinquent and problem behavior.

Youth courts frequently involve a lot of positive adult-youth interaction, too. Many service clubs, local businesses, and governments get involved, providing training and community service opportunities. Youth feel empowered by helping others; adults change their views of challenging youth.

Find Out More

National Association of Youth Courts
youthcourt.net

HEALTH CARE

Two ways of involving youth seem to have an impact on reducing teen pregnancy:

INCREASE SERVICE LEARNING OPPORTUNITIES—*Emerging Answers 2007* cites a study that found that some service learning programs delayed the initiation of sex among middle school students. Three other studies that evaluated different programs in multiple locations also found that **service learning reduced pregnancy rates during the academic year in which the teens were involved.** The programs differed considerably, indicating that it was not the content of the curriculum that made the difference. However, all of the programs were intensive and involved students for many hours (e.g., 40 to 80 hours through the academic year) after school.

INVOLVE YOUTH AS TRAINERS IN PREVENTION PROGRAMS—The Postponing Sexual Involvement for Young Teens program (PSI) grew out of Dr. Marion Howard's research in the 1980s, which showed that young people were steadily exposed to sexual messages through television, advertising, movies, and popular music lyrics. PSI is designed to supplement existing human sexuality curriculums so youth can get information *and* build resistance skills. A key component of PSI's success is that **teens teach the education sessions**. Besides benefiting from leadership and serving as role models, teens find it easier to talk to each other about topics such as how to say no without hurting someone's feelings. An evaluation of a PSI program involving 536 low-income, mostly Black 8th graders in Atlanta showed that participating youth had higher rates of contraceptive use, less-frequent sex, and delayed initiation of sex compared to youth who didn't participate in the program.

Activate Sectors

What This Means
Motivate all community groups—schools, faith-based organizations, youth, businesses, human services, and health-care organizations—to create an asset-building culture and to contribute fully to young people's healthy development.

The Goal
Bring different sectors together around a common vision of healthy development for all young people.

Chances are you're already connected to many different sectors in your community as a result of the prevention work you're doing. Collaborating to share missions, resources, and ideas makes it possible to reduce duplication of services and maximize resources.

Working in partnership also allows you to do something very important: focus on improving the environment in which young people live. While it's important to work on building assets in youth, genuine, long-lasting change will not happen until we can make an impact on the culture and context around them.

We know there are many different youth development efforts going on in communities all over the United States and Canada using the Developmental Assets framework, as well as those that use other valid, useful frameworks such as Communities That Care (CTC), America's Promise, Asset-Based Community Development (ABCD), and the Strategic Prevention Framework (SPF) developed by the U.S. government's Substance Abuse and Mental Health Services Administration (SAMHSA). **Search Institute's approach to infusing assets into prevention programs and strategies is meant to be complementary to other efforts because we know many practitioners are using multiple approaches.** Multiple approaches benefit young people and communities.

You can use the asset framework as a common language when working with other groups. Many prevention programs successfully blend their approaches and translate asset-oriented goals and plans into language that satisfies accountability criteria for a variety of funders and other stakeholders.

For example, here's a diagram that shows the relationship between asset-building activities and SAMHSA's Strategic Prevention Framework tasks:

SAMHSA Strategic Prevention Framework (SPF) Tasks & Asset Activities						
SPF Tasks	Conduct a community needs assessment	Mobilize and/or build capacity	Develop a comprehensive strategic plan	Implement evidence-based prevention activities	Monitor process, evaluate effectiveness
Asset Activities	Develop community-wide profile of Developmental Assets, risk behaviors, and thriving indicators	Create cross-sector and intergenerational leadership teams Build shared vision Disseminate vision and profile to the community	In response to vision and profile, blend community-wide asset-building initiative with prevention programs	Launch, monitor, and refine coordinated rollout of prevention programs within a community-wide asset-building initiative	Conduct change-over-time assessments of youth asset levels, youth risk behaviors, thriving indicators, community indicators

Here are some strategies to help activate sectors and strengthen your prevention programs.

SCHOOLS

SPEAK THE SAME LANGUAGE—Many schools provide substance-abuse education. To increase the effectiveness of the message, parents, faith communities, and youth organizations should join together to promote consistent messages to young people throughout the community. For example, many communities are working on simply educating parents and other adults that it's against the law to provide alcohol to minors. The school superintendent and local police chief in Bellevue, Washington, sent joint letters to all parents in the district reminding them of existing alcohol-related laws *and* the penalties for breaking them.

ENGAGE FAMILIES—A study published by the Southwest Educational Development Laboratory confirms that when schools engage families in ways that are linked to improved learning, and support parent involvement at home and school, students make greater gains. **The better young people do in school, the more likely they'll avoid risky behaviors.** Teacher outreach to parents was identified as particularly powerful in producing stronger, more consistent gains in student performance in reading and math. Effective outreach practices include face-to-face meetings, sending learning materials home, keeping in touch about programs, and workshops for parents on helping children at home.

PROVIDE LEADERSHIP—To build assets systemwide, the Association of Alaska School Boards (AASB) initiated a comprehensive school improvement program called Quality Schools/Quality Students (QS2). Successes so far include districts meeting No Child Left Behind annual progress benchmarks, fewer youth involved in risky behaviors, and improved reading skills. Strategies include:

Find Out More

Southwest Educational Development Laboratory
"A New Wave of Evidence: The Impact of School, Family, and Community Connections on Student Achievement" (2002).
sedl.org

- Connecting Commonalities. AASB staff guide districts through strategic planning, which involves a varied group of active members working together to create a common vision and unified effort for youth success.

- Embedding Assets. Build both school improvement *and* active community engagement with an eye toward incorporating both strategies in the fabric of diverse communities so they continue once the formal QS2 partnership is over.

- Speaking the Same Language. School staff, parents, and community members are taught to speak the same daily language about assets.

YOUTH-SERVING ORGANIZATIONS

Prevention Partners for Youth Development (PPYD) in Syracuse, New York, is an asset-building community coalition of county organizations, neighborhoods, and individuals including youth. The coalition focuses on educating and mobilizing the community to build assets for and with youth ages 12 to 21. Some of its key strategies include:

CONVENING QUARTERLY NETWORKING MEETINGS—The coalition meets regularly and focuses meetings on helping all coalition participants better understand principles of positive youth development and how to use them in their organizations.

USING A COMMUNITY CAPACITY-BUILDING TRAINING TEAM—They bring together youth and citizens with special expertise to help youth-serving organizations integrate youth development principles into their everyday work.

INCLUDING YOUTH AS PARTNERS IN EVALUATION—The coalition created a program where young people both develop and conduct surveys with local organizations and community leaders to measure project impact and use the results to refine programs even further.

Find Out More
Prevention Partners for Youth Development
ppyd.org

FAMILY-SERVING ORGANIZATIONS

Under the umbrella of the Association of Alaska School Boards' Initiative for Community Engagement—Alaska ICE for short—many faith organizations have become active partners in asset building for prevention. Consider some of these activities:

CELEBRATE DIVERSITY—Working with Alaska ICE, a broad group of Juneau residents, including faith communities, put on a successful community-wide Diversity Week celebration. Joining were artists, media, schools, the city, native and ethnic organizations, businesses, and lots of youth and adults.

REDUCE BARRIERS—Alaska ICE partnered with the State of Alaska Office of Faith-Based and Community Initiatives to put on a Faith Information Day—Passport to Understanding to break down barriers of misinformation and misunderstanding and for youth to learn about diverse faith practices.

ENCOURAGE SERVICE—Alaska ICE offers small stipends to faith communities to support youth-adult community service projects as well as training about how faith communities can incorporate sustained asset building into their work.

Find Out More
Alaska ICE
alaskaice.org

JUVENILE JUSTICE

The Family Relations Division of the Allen Superior Court in Fort Wayne, Indiana, began to shift its focus from risk identification to positive youth development in 1997. Now people from all disciplines are involved in the community initiative that grew out of the court's efforts, and 700 people regularly attend the county court's Annual Conference on Youth.

Assets are infused into every aspect of the court's work, including interactions with foster families, health and human services, juvenile probation, law enforcement, schools, and health agencies. Among some of the court's innovative practices:

CREATING A COMMUNITY-WIDE SOCIAL MAP—To identify drug-dealing hot spots, transportation insufficiencies, and neighborhood bullies, the court created a community map that showed those geographic areas. The map helps to inform the court of barriers confronting families and youth. It also shows available social services and is shared with other youth- and family-serving organizations.

TEACHING LOCAL AGENCIES—The court partnered with the Foellinger Foundation to further integrate Developmental Assets and strength-based procedures into the community and train local agencies in the use of the assets model in their existing programs.

DEVELOPING A "CIRCLE OF CARE"—The court identified the needs of families and children who appeared in court and provided strength-based resources.

HEALTH

A number of community initiatives are using asset building, prevention grants, and risk reduction in creative ways to bring many sectors together on behalf of youth. For example, the Upper Bucks Healthy Communities • Healthy Youth Coalition in Upper Bucks, Pennsylvania, can document a 15 percent reduction in tobacco use among 12th graders, a 5 percent decrease in alcohol use among 10th graders, and a 44 percent reduction in tobacco use among 8th graders. They reached multiple sectors with these strategies:

LAUNCHING A SOCIAL NORMS CAMPAIGN—The campaign, which took place in one middle school and three high schools, was aimed at informing youth and parents that a majority of teens in Upper Bucks choose *not* to drink; the coalition recruited 65 youth from all three high schools to form a "street team" to help plan and implement the campaign.

RECRUITING AND TRAINING YOUTH SPORTS COACHES—To help reduce substance abuse, the coaches attended Positive Coaching Alliance workshops called Double Goal Coach, which taught them how to integrate positive youth development strategies into their coaching.

PARTNERING WITH BUSINESSES—The coalition worked with places like Burger King restaurants, which learned youth were selling drugs outside some of its stores. The partnership helped raise money to train adult professionals who work with youth and families.

Find Out More
Upper Bucks HC • HY Coalition
justcommunity.com

Influence Civic Decisions

What This Means
Influence decision makers and opinion leaders to contribute financial, media, and policy resources in support of positive transformation of communities and society.

The Goal
Focus community strategies on changing the environment for all young people.

It takes a lot of effort to keep prevention programs going. Even when we have proof of our effectiveness in hand, sometimes resources dry up, political winds shift, or community concerns change. The more opportunities you can take to plan, implement, and evaluate effective, asset-centered programs, the better your chances of ensuring that young people get the support they need. Finding ways to widen the circles of connection and influence you have with other stakeholders in your communities will allow you to spread the message about the good work you're doing as well as build strong partnerships to help sustain your work.

Creating asset-attentive communities comes through mobilizing public will, power, capacity, and commitment to create a culture in which all citizens are expected to contribute to the healthy development of young people. This must be done intentionally, but it can be done both formally and informally.

Consider these overarching strategies to help you strengthen and sustain your work throughout the entire community:

UNITE VISION AND ACTION—Tout a shared vision that unites multiple sectors, systems, policies, and leaders across political, ideological, religious, economic, and ethnic differences. Share an existing vision more widely or, if none exists, be the catalyst to get the conversation started.

RECRUIT AND CONNECT ASSET CHAMPIONS—Nurture relationships with those who naturally champion the asset framework—people who have the passion to spread the word and help make a vision a reality. Create opportunities for these champions to learn from, support, and inspire each other.

MAKE YOUTH INVOLVEMENT NORMATIVE—Young people should be involved anywhere and everywhere they can. The more visible they are in communities—describing issues of importance to them and sharing solutions—the more others will pay attention. Many cities now have youth boards, and youth are being invited to join school boards.

Find Out More

National League of Cities
nlc.org

....

Find Out More

Facilitator's Guide for Participatory Evaluation with Young People, ssw.umich.edu/public/currentProjects/youthAndCommunity/

The Program for Youth and Community at the University of Michigan School of Social Work has produced a workbook and a facilitator's guide to participatory evaluation with young people.

....

USE POLICY PANELS TO EFFECT LARGER-SCALE COMMUNITY CHANGE—Community leaders in San Diego, California, established a county-level policy panel to help tackle underage drinking problems. The panel represents a cross-section of leadership and was founded on the principle that underage drinking needs to be addressed largely by the adults who determine the circumstances in which alcohol is available. They have successfully launched public information campaigns, lobbied for drinking bans at parks and beaches, and influenced the city council to increase penalties for adults who provide alcohol to minors.

EMBED ASSETS INTO PLANS AND POLICIES—Communities are working to embed asset language and approaches in adolescent health plans, violence prevention plans, and suicide prevention plans. Some communities implement youth master plans, which help cities identify and fund priorities important to youth.

The National League of Cities joined with America's Promise to develop *A City Platform for Strengthening Families and Improving Outcomes for Children and Youth,* which the league now encourages municipal leaders to adopt. The platform outlines 21 action steps to help improve the lives of youth and families, including such activities as enlisting youth to map local resources and needs, and supporting other youth-led service activities that tap the potential of young people as community assets.

GET GOOD RESULTS—There's no better way to achieve sustainability in your work than getting good outcomes. Invest in innovation, research, and evaluation. Getting youth to participate in your evaluation provides more opportunities for youth involvement and adds to your effectiveness and credibility.

SPREAD THE WORD—Once you've got good results, get the word out! Activate the usual channels like newspapers and television whenever you can, but think creatively when it comes to sharing your successes. Communicate through parks and recreation directories, local foundation or faith-based newsletters, or other agency Web sites.

Better yet, partner with youth to communicate. The Alaska Teen Media Institute (ATMI) trains young people in journalism skills who then work to promote the teen perspective in print media and radio. Youth are heard regularly on Anchorage radio stations and statewide over the Alaska Public Radio Network. They even produce their own monthly half-hour teen-oriented show called *In Other News.*

Resources

In addition to the many resources cited throughout this guide, here are other useful materials to help strengthen your work.

American Bar Association National Teen Dating Violence Prevention Initiative (abanet.org)

Building Bridges to Benefit Youth, National Collaboration for Youth & National Juvenile Justice Network (nassembly.org)

Emerging Answers 2007: Research on Programs to Reduce Teen Pregnancy and Sexually Transmitted Diseases (The National Campaign to Prevent Teen and Unplanned Pregnancy, 2007), by Douglas Kirby, Ph.D. (teenpregnancy.org)

"Improving the Health of Young Canadians," Canadian Institute for Health Information, 2005 (cihi.ca)

National Education Association, drug prevention resources online, including events and lesson plans (nea.org)

Preventing Underage Drinking: Using the SAMHSA Strategic Prevention Framework and Getting to Outcomes to Achieve Results, by Pamela Imm, Matthew Chinman, and Abraham Wandersman, in collaboration with Join Together, School of Public Health, Boston University (rand.org/pubs/)

Search Institute (search-institute.org)

Getting to Outcomes with Developmental Assets: Ten Steps to Measuring Success in Youth Programs and Communities by Deborah Fisher, Pamela Imm, Matthew Chinman, and Abe Wandersman

Great Places to Learn: Creating Asset-Building Schools That Help Students Succeed by Clay Roberts, Peter C. Scales, and Neal Starkman

Helping Teens Handle Tough Experiences: Strategies to Foster Resilience by Jill Nelson and Sarah Kjos

More Than Just a Place To Go: How Developmental Assets Can Strengthen Your Youth Program by Kristin Johnstad, James Conway, and Yvonne Pearson

A Quick-Start Guide to Building Assets in Your School by Deborah Davis and Lisa Race

Research findings published online in *Insights & Evidence* (search-institute.org/downloads):

"Positive Youth Development So Far: Core Hypotheses and Their Implications for Policy and Practice" (Nov. 2006, Vol. 3, #1)

"Sorting Out What Makes a Difference" (Oct. 2007, Vol. 4, #1).

"Tapping the Power of Community: Building Assets to Strengthen Substance Abuse Prevention" (March 2004, Vol. 2, #1)

U.S. Departments of Education, Justice, and Health and Human Services

Center for Substance Abuse Prevention (prevention.samhsa.gov)

Community Anti-Drug Coalitions of America (cadca.org)

Office of Juvenile Justice and Delinquency Prevention (ojjdp.ncjrs.org)

Office of National Drug Control Policy (whitehousedrugpolicy.gov)

Office of Safe and Drug-Free Schools (ed.gov/about/offices/list/osdfs)

SAMHSA's National Clearinghouse for Alcohol and Drug Information (ncadi.samhsa.gov)

Acknowledgments

I've been writing for Search Institute for more than a decade, which has allowed me the opportunity to pick the brains of many experienced, talented, and wise people. The only credit I take for the material in this book is being the scribe who helped articulate the best ideas of others. My continual thanks to these dedicated asset builders whose words, thoughts, ideas, and advice inform much of what I do and most of what you see here:

Shelby Andress	Derek Peterson
Chris Beyer	Clay Roberts
Peter Benson	Patsy Roybal
Matthew Chinman	Lee Rush
Michael Clark	Peter Scales
María Guajardo Lucero	Neal Starkman
Pamela Imm	Abe Wandersman
Becky Judd	And all of my colleagues at Vision Training Associates
Ruth Lindegarde	

I also would like to thank authors Deborah Davis and Lisa Race, who did such a fine job on *A Quick-Start Guide to Building Assets in Your Schools,* which made my work on this guide so much easier.

About the Author

Deborah Fisher is an author with more than 30 years experience in print and online magazine work, project management, and nonfiction books. A former Minnesota Public Radio legal affairs reporter and NPR contributor, she now specializes in writing and training for Search Institute.

Deborah has worked with many Puget Sound organizations to design and implement asset-based projects, including reducing youth violence, starting family support centers and Healthy Communities • Healthy Youth initiatives, and teaching asset development to youth workers and community members.

As a national trainer for Vision Training Associates, Deborah works with communities to plan, implement, and evaluate asset programs and initiatives. www.deborahfisher.org